WE GOT YOU BACK

Heaven Can Wait

Lourdes "Lulu" R. Mercado

ISBN 979-8-89243-723-3 (paperback)
ISBN 979-8-89243-724-0 (digital)

Copyright © 2024 by Lourdes "Lulu" R. Mercado

All rights reserved. No part of this publication may be reproduced, distributed, or transmitted in any form or by any means, including photocopying, recording, or other electronic or mechanical methods without the prior written permission of the publisher. For permission requests, solicit the publisher via the address below.

Christian Faith Publishing
832 Park Avenue
Meadville, PA 16335
www.christianfaithpublishing.com

Printed in the United States of America

CONTENTS

Foreword v
Chapter 1—We Got You Back 1
Chapter 2—Baby 12
Chapter 3—Professor Lulu....................................18
Chapter 4—My First Love 23
Chapter 5—Life in the USA 28
Chapter 6—All My Children 32
Chapter 7—Career Woman 44
Chapter 8—The Love of My Life 48
Chapter 9—Losing Vic 53
Chapter 10—Grief and Sickness 60
Chapter 11—Life Began at 72..............................65
Giving...81
Acknowledgment 83

FOREWORD

Lourdes (Lulu) R. Mercado, a Filipina, moved to America to be with her husband, Vic. They started a family and were blessed with four beautiful children. She was a working mother. Balancing parenthood and a career requires effective time management, prioritization, and a strong support system. She worked as an accountant at Universal Studios, tour accounting before she became a realtor, then a real estate broker. She owned and operated different real estate franchises with the help and support of her husband and friends who trusted her to partner with her. In spite of operating her own real estate office and mortgage brokerage with unwavering diligence, life presented unexpected challenges along the way. Three cancers she fought with all her might and a near-death experience—a perilous sight—and the passing of Vic, the love of her life. After Vic passed away, she had many health issues; but Lulu was determined to keep on living, fulfill her purpose, and keep on giving. Her name was given to her in honor of Our Lady of Lourdes. She thought Mary's healing miracle had been working through her all those years. Dealing with cancer multiple times was incredibly challenging. Her resilience and strength were a sight to behold. A true inspiration, as her story was told, she refused to let her illness define her fate and lived every day, refusing to wait. Lulu believed she had much more to give and that her purpose in life was yet to live. Her unwavering spirit and positive vibe inspired all around her to thrive. Her story reminds us to never give in and to keep pushing forward through thick and thin. Lulu's journey is a testament to living life to the fullest and never falling.

CHAPTER 1

We Got You Back

October 3, 2019—little after 1:00 a.m.

I woke up with a cough. I had a perpetual cough during the winter season, but when I woke up, I knew that this was something different. I had trouble breathing and felt something big in the back of my throat.

    I quickly ran to the bathroom, and luckily, I made it to the toilet. I threw up blood and filled it to the brim. The toilet was full of my own blood. I had no time to react; I had to flush the toilet so I could throw up again. In no time, the toilet became filled with blood again. I was dizzy and disoriented. The only thing I could think to do was to look for another bowl to throw up in. Instead of finding a bowl, I ran to my cell phone that was on my dresser next to my bed and called 911. I began to have shortness of breath, finding it almost impossible to breathe. I told the dispatcher, "I need help, please." I gave her my address and told her my name and that I was going to try to unlock the door. Holding onto the staircase railing, I couldn't stand anymore. I needed to sit down, and I lowered myself to the steps. One step at a time, I sat on the top of my stairs and scooted down the stairway, with a cell phone in one hand and a towel full of blood in the other. I finally made it down to the bottom of the staircase, to the door, and unlocked it.

I collapsed, falling on my tile floor. I was in my home and alone.

The next day, I woke up and found myself in a hospital bed connected to a lot of medical machines. I was told that I had lost a lot of blood and needed a blood transfusion. When I was finally conscious, I was so tired all I wanted to do was sleep. I remember nurses coming into my room and using medical suctions to remove fluid from my throat. I was attached to a ventilator that was helping me breathe. It was keeping me alive. I remember constantly being prodded. The nursing staff performed an endless amount of X-rays and lab work on me. They stuck needles in me countless times a day to check my blood. I didn't know what had happened, but I knew they were working hard to figure it out.

I remember being visited by a male doctor with glasses, wearing a white coat. "*We got you back*," he said with a warm smile and a sense of reassurance.

I was so tired I closed my eyes without hearing anything else and fell back asleep. The next time I woke up, I saw my eldest son, VJ, walking around the room. He looked worried but happy to see me. He said it reminded him of when he saw his dad on a ventilator three years ago. I felt so happy to see him. I looked around and saw my youngest daughter, Jamie. My eyes began to fill up with tears, and I was so thankful to see my children by my side. I realized I was in the same hospital as my husband, Vic, before he passed away from a stroke three years ago. I didn't know if I was going to make it out. I was so scared, but I left it up to God. I didn't remember much after that.

A few days later, I woke up and found myself in another room. They had transported me to Kaiser Hospital in Woodland Hills. I was awake longer as the days passed. My two other children, Lori and Vicky, came to see me. Vicky flew all the way from Canada. My children were all there and were all worried about me. They tried to reassure me that I was doing well and I would be alright. Vicky talked to the doctors to find out as much information as she could. She told me I had lost over sixteen pints of blood and that the doctors couldn't believe I had survived. They thought it was a miracle. The longer I was awake, the more I could feel a plastic tube down my throat. Every time the nurses needed to move it for whatever reason, it became more and more uncomfortable. It was unbearable. They had to suck the fluid that was filling up inside my windpipe; it felt excruciatingly painful. I was uncomfortable and groggy. I couldn't speak with the tube down my throat. I felt so helpless.

As I was getting my strength back and staying awake longer each day, I was tasked with proving to the doctors that I could breathe on my own. It was the only way I could get the ventilator out. The nurses would give me tips on how to breathe on my own so that they could remove the ventilator. They were telling me to take long, deep breaths. My youngest daughter, Jamie, tried to help me relax and would guide me in taking long, deep breaths. Though I was trying, I became more and more frustrated with myself and sad that I wasn't able to prove to them that I could breathe on my own. After what seemed like forever, I was able to hold my breath long enough, in front of the doctor, that he finally permitted the nurses to remove the ventilator. Victory! I did it. For the first time in days, I felt hopeful I would get out of the hospital soon.

At the time the ventilator was removed, Vicky was at the store, and Jamie messaged her the good news. Vicky was so excited she told me she jumped with joy at the store. People around her were startled and intrigued. Vicky told complete strangers about what happened to me and my success, and they were happy for me. I remember Vicky spending countless nights sleeping with me in the hospital room during my recovery. After a week, I finally told her to go back to my house to get a good night's sleep in a bed, instead of the hard, uncomfortable hospital chair she had been sleeping in all week. Only after all the nurses and doctors reassured her that I was steadily on the road to recovery, Vicky accepted the offer and headed back to my house.

During dry summer nights in California, the San Fernando Valley is notorious for sudden brush fires sparking up out of nowhere, particularly up in the windy part of the hills where we live. That night, Vicky drove to my house in Porter Ranch (a suburb of the Valley) and received an "Emergency Alert" on her cell phone, advising about a violent brush fire that was quickly picking up speed in Sylmar, a small suburb just east of Porter Ranch. Since the fire was still on the other side of the 210 freeway at that time, Vicky figured she was safe at my house. She thought, *What are the chances of the brush fire hopping a whole freeway to endanger anyone in our neighborhood?* So she pulled up to my house and quickly fell asleep in my bed, exhausted from the emotionally draining week she had at the hospital with me.

Around 3:00 a.m. California time, Vicky's husband, Greg, who was awake on the East Coast in

Canada (it was 6:00 a.m. there), saw on the news that our neighborhood, Porter Ranch, was quickly being engulfed by this brush fire. Vicky's husband called her as soon as he saw the news to make sure she was safe. Vicky woke up to his call and was disoriented from the smoke and heat. Greg was terrified for her safety and told her she needed to leave my house immediately, because he could see on the news that the fire was getting closer and closer to my neighborhood. Vicky opened my bedroom door and the room quickly filled up with smoke. She ran to the window to look outside and saw the dark night's sky was consumed with ash and smoke. In a panic, Vicky quickly rushed to pack up as many of her things as she could before leaving the house.

Vicky quickly threw everything in the car and just started driving. At that point, she had no idea where she was going. She just knew she had to get as far away from the fire as she could but still be close to the hospital, where I was. She ended up staying with her cousin May and May's partner David. After a few days, when the fire was under control and once the police deemed it was safe to return, Vicky finally went back to the house.

While I was in the hospital recovering, I was grateful I was able to eat again, but I didn't like the hospital food. (Who does?) I was weak and I didn't want to see anyone but my kids. I didn't want to answer any questions or have people see me not put together, helpless and vulnerable. As soon as I got my strength back, I asked my kids to give me my phone and I started working, making deals, and answering emails. I found out a good friend and realtor in my office passed away from a heart attack. I was surprised and sad. I called his wife immediately and extended my sympathy. I understood what it was like to lose a husband. I tried to assure her the best I could, reminding her that she has family and friends by her side and that her two sons will be okay. She was grateful, but I could tell she was still hurting. I knew her loss; she was experiencing an emptiness and pain I am all too familiar with.

    I was staying in two different hospitals over the course of three weeks. After lying in hospital beds, undergoing countless medical tests, it felt so good to hear the doctor tell me that I was well enough to go home. It was like a huge weight had lifted. At the time I was ready to be discharged, our home was full of smoke and ashes. Thankfully, the fire in the neighborhood didn't harm anyone or destroy my home, but I couldn't stay there to recuperate because the air quality was so bad. I didn't want to go to a rehabilitation facility; I wanted to be with my kids.

My kids had a meeting and decided that the best place for me to recuperate was with my daughter, Lori, and her husband, Eric, and their two young kids in Long Beach. I stayed with Lori and her family for four weeks. It was a joyous experience to be with my grandchildren, Ethan and Charlie. Charlie started calling me "Granny." I got to be a grandmother to them. I cooked them spaghetti one evening, and Charlie didn't want sauce with the spaghetti and started to cry. Ethan said, "Charlie, don't cry over spaghetti sauce." Ethan was older and wanted to show that they were grateful. I realized they were so smart, respectful, and kind. I was impressed that they did their chores without being asked. Charlie would clean the table after dinner and Ethan took out the trash. I spent the nights sharing the bed with Charlie. It reminded me of putting my children to bed when they were young. It was great that I could do the "grandmother things" for them, and I continued to work remotely. I was in touch with realtors, office staff, and clients.

I was in the hospital bed for so long; I needed to strengthen my body. I needed to learn how to walk on my own again. I had a physical therapist who came to Lori's house. I first learned how to walk with a cane. I didn't like it. I wasn't used to it, and I had trouble balancing. The physical therapists encouraged me to use the cane, in case I would fall. I had three different therapists who came to the house. They even brought me the walker that I used in the hospital. Fortunately, I didn't need to use it. I met with a physical therapist twice a week for three long weeks. I felt like I really didn't need them, but I was grateful they were there to make sure I was on the right track toward recovery.

My children made sure my house in Porter Ranch was cleaned from all the ash and soot that had settled into my curtains and furniture before I got home. The remnants from the fire could have been dangerous to my recovery, but luckily, I was okay to be home again. My youngest daughter, Jamie, stayed with me.

It was so nice to be back in my own home again, I had more time to think about what happened to me. The phrase that stuck with me was the doctor telling me, "*We got you back.*" *Where did I go?* I thought. Was I given a second chance at life? Did I still have more work to do on earth, with lessons to share and life to live? I had an overwhelming sense of renewed energy and purpose and a desire to make the most of the time I have been given.

I reflected on my passions and interests. I wanted to make positive changes and pursue new goals. Each person's purpose and the work they have to do on earth is unique and deeply personal. For me, I realized the most important thing in the world was my family. I was so grateful for them and the moments together. I was grateful I got to be a mother to my children and see them grow and change. I was grateful to be a grandmother and see my grandchildren's personalities and interests take shape. I was able to appreciate the opportunities and blessings that came my way. I volunteered for causes I cared about, and I found ways to support my community.

I felt writing a book, telling my story would help others and their life journey. I hesitated, I thought, *Would people want to read my book? Is my life interesting to share?* I was encouraged and supported by my children. I was reminded by my "why": I wanted my grandchildren and my great-grandchildren to learn about me and where they came from. I wanted them to know the challenges I faced and overcame so that they could believe in themselves. I share my story so they, too, can have faith.

CHAPTER 2

Baby

I was born Cecilia Sanchez Regular to Cesar Regular and Virginia "Nena" Sanchez. At my baptism, my parents decided to change my name to Lourdes. I suspect it was because of my mom's devotion to Our Lady of Lourdes.

My mommy's dad came from Spain, and he was a photographer when he met my grandmother. My grandparents passed away when my mommy and her siblings were in their teens. After their death, my mommy and her sister, Mama Elia, went to live in a dormitory run by nuns. Their brother, Papa Jimmy, went to a dormitory run by priests. After a few years, their inheritance was mishandled by the administrator, so they left the dormitories and returned to their province, Masbate, without finishing their school. There, in Masbate, at the age of seventeen, my mommy met my dad, who was twenty-four and an engineer. My dad had a younger brother, Sergio, with two children.

My dad had three engineering degrees: civil, sanitary, and contractor management. I was told that he was the first engineer in Masbate, our Visayan province in the Philippines. He joined the US Army and retired as a captain. While serving, he fought in WWII during the Japanese Occupation of the Philippines. Like my husband, Vic's dad, our fathers were both imprisoned and survived the Bataan Death March. My dad was a professor at the Mapua Institute of Technology in the Philippines.

He was later assigned to Davao as regional director for real property and management. My dad was an honest man. Working for the government, he was offered many corrupt deals, but he didn't take any of them.

I was told by my older siblings that our parents' qualities of honesty and kindness were passed on to their children. Honesty and kindness are values I hope to have instilled in my children. It has built trust and strengthened my relationship with family, friends, and coworkers. I live by being transparent and authentic in everything I do.

Kindness and compassion contribute to a harmonious and compassionate society. Acts of kindness, both big and small, can have a profound impact on the lives of others that we can't even imagine. Simple gestures such as lending a listening ear, offering a helping hand, or showing empathy and understanding can make a significant difference in someone's day or even their life. I'm grateful I got to see my parents show great kindness and compassion growing up.

As my siblings and I were growing up, my family's house was always filled with relatives from the province. They would stay in our house temporarily to go to school in Manila. My parents were very warm and welcoming. They shared what they had and were always there for those who needed support.

Before I was born, my parents moved a lot because my father was in the military. I was number eleven out of twelve children, and I was a daddy's girl. My mother stayed at home to take care of us. When I was growing up, the first beach I went to swim in was in Cavite, where my husband, Vic, was born and raised. My brother Vicente, my sister Elia, and I were the three youngest siblings at that time and were left in the home while my elder siblings had already moved out to raise their own families. As a child, I liked to play hide-and-seek with the girls living in my neighborhood. We played marbles and *piko*, a Filipino variation of the game hopscotch. I remember how my dad was so strict when my siblings and I were growing up, and my brothers would be mischievous in trying to break the rules of the house. My dad did not want anyone to smoke cigarettes, so my brother, Raphael (whom we called Paeng), would hide in the bathroom to smoke. When my dad would want to use the bathroom, my brother would put the cigarette in his mouth. My brothers were finding creative ways to not follow the house rules. I did not think twice about disobeying my parents. I was a good girl and a good student. I would walk to church regularly on my own. After school, I would stop by the church on my way home from school and pray.

When my dad taught engineering at Mapua Institute of Technology, he would have me correct his students' quizzes. I was thirteen years old at the time. My cousin and I would review his students' papers to correct them.

In my early teens, my father was assigned to work in Davao. I spent my first three years of high school there. My father would always come home from work for lunch and take a nap during his break time. One afternoon, he came home from work to take a nap just like he always did. I was in the other bedroom when I heard my mom panicking. I went to their room, and I could see my dad sitting up, but it looked like he could not get out of bed. My mother called his office staff for help. In twenty minutes, they were at the house and they quickly brought him to the hospital. We found out that he had a stroke. All my brothers and sisters from different places in the Philippines rushed to the hospital. I would visit him every day after school and would find him unconscious. I would talk to him about my day and hope that he would hear me and would wake up. I would cry and pray and beg him to wake up. My mom was by his side every day. But he never woke up; he passed away after a week of being unconscious in the hospital. I experienced exactly the same thing with Vic when he had a stroke and never woke up after seven days.

All our family visited and were by my dad's bedside until his death. He was brought back to Manila for his burial. Being an officer of the US Army, he was flown on a government aircraft to Manila. My mom and a few of my siblings flew back with his remains. After my dad was put to rest, I went back to Davao to finish my third year of high school, Mindanao College, which is now called the University of Mindanao. Following my third year of high school, I went back to Manila to be with my mother and my other siblings. I finished my high school and graduated from Saint Anne's Academy. I was sad during my high school graduation because I missed my father very much. I knew he would have been very proud of me. After graduation, I stayed to live in Green Hills with my mother. Little did I know that I would meet my future husband there seven years later.

CHAPTER 3

Professor Lulu

I went to an all-girls college, Philippine Women's University in Manila, the first university for women in Asia founded by Asians. I wanted to study psychology, but I thought it would be hard to get a job, so I got my degree in business administration and majored in accounting.

After graduating college, I went to school to get my master's in business administration at the University of Santo Tomas in Manila, but because of my unexpected travel to the United States, I was not able to finish it.

I taught accounting for college students at Santa Catalina College, an all-girls school run by nuns. The principal was a large Filipina woman in her fifties, and she wore a white habit. My first time meeting her was when I was interviewing to be their accounting instructor. I felt competent for the job. During the interview, she was very kind and warm. Though I wasn't nervous, she made me feel more at ease and comfortable as she asked me questions about my life and qualifications to be a teacher. She was impressed that I was on the dean's list and that I was continuing my studies. At the time, I was enrolled to get my master's degree in business administration. After the interview was over, I was confident that she liked me. The next day, she called to offer me the job. I was excited, honored, and humbled that I was going to teach college students who were not much younger than me.

My office was the classroom. I had a blackboard behind me, and my students lined up in their chairs in front of me. I taught them the basics of accounting and bookkeeping. Since we were close in age, they treated me like their friend and not a teacher. At that time, we would gather at people's houses and dance to American hits, like the Beatles, and eat Filipino food. I went to their parties and chatted with my students outside the classroom. I was close to them and met their family members.

I loved my job. I loved getting paid. It felt good to earn money on my own. I liked being in front of a large group of people. I remember I wore a yellow blazer pantsuit often. Yellow was my favorite color, and I felt happy and confident wearing it. I was a career woman and furthering my education. I think that was why my husband was impressed. My life as a professor was cut short, however. Meeting my future husband would take me away from the nuns and college students in the small town of Legarda, Philippines, to the big city of Los Angeles, California.

AN INTERVIEW

Keen observant eyes won't fail to notice a new face coming out of a classroom, smiling in spite of the hectic time she's been through. Heads are turned to her direction whenever she passes by. Our college is indeed fortunate to be given the services of this sweet-faced lady, Miss Lourdes Regular.

Miss Regular was born to Cesario Regular who died when she was in third year high school, and Virginia Sanchez both of Masbate, on June 6. She is the youngest of the girls in the family of twelve children consisting of six girls and six boys.

Charm is not the only asset of Miss Regular for she has the brains as well. She graduated with honors in elementary and placed third honor when she was in high school. She pursued her college at Philippine Women's University where she was a consistent scholar. At present she is taking up her Masters in Business Administration at the University of Santo Tomas.

After a feverish day of teaching and studying she tries to relax by watching the television specially on Sunday which is her only free day. She loves long-stemmed roses and the colors yellow and green are appealing to her eyes.

She finds teaching profession very challenging yet rewarding. She likes Sta. Catalina girls for their friendliness. Her three aspirations in life are to earn a living enough for herself and her family, to be able to contribute something for the development of our country, and to get married to the right man at the right time, and raise a happy family.

When asked her opinion regarding the mini skirt she amazingly revealed that it's okey provided it is properly worn in the right occasion. Our dear mentor believes in long engagement for it gives the couple the chance to know each other better. She is not against going steady at early age provided the persons concerned are matured enough to know and understand love.

That's Miss Regular… An asset to the teaching profession.

JOJIE A. COBARRUBIAS
Santa Catalina Student

CHAPTER 4

My First Love

I met my husband, Vic Daza Mercado, in March of 1971 at my aunt Tita Conching's house in Greenhills. Greenhills was one of the most prestigious places in Manila. It was Lent season, and she hosted a reading for the Passion of Christ for her family and friends during Holy Week. While everyone was preparing for the resurrection of our Lord Jesus, I was preparing for my life to change. I was introduced to a group of young male professionals who worked at Subic Base Olongapo City, Philippines. Vic was one of the young professionals. I chatted with Vic about my family, work, and school. I could tell he liked me; he kept asking questions about my life and didn't want me to leave his side. We talked the entire night by the poolside until the party ended. We were the last ones there. At that time in the Philippines, families wouldn't let their daughters out of the house without someone to accompany them. I had my nephew, Manny, with me. He was nine years old and my "chaperone." He was so bored he fell asleep while Vic and I talked the night away. Vic ended up getting my phone number from a family friend and called me the next day. He told me he was leaving for California in May, which was two months after we first met. He wanted to join his brothers and sister in the United States to find better opportunities.

When Vic told me, I didn't care that he was about to leave the country. I was so busy teaching and attending school to get my master's in business administration that I didn't think twice about Vic or a possible future with him. As soon as he arrived in the US, he sent me a postcard. I responded to it. Later on, he told me it made him so happy and gave him hope to continue our friendship. He started calling me long-distance and sending me love letters. I didn't know at the time, but he already had a girlfriend in the Philippines. Eventually, he told her that he could no longer continue their relationship. He wanted to be with me.

For months, I would rush home after work excited to receive Vic's letters, and I waited to talk to him on the phone. It was a fifteen-hour time difference, and I would wait by the phone anticipating his call. During our long-distance courtship, I fell in love. I felt like he was the only man for me. He had a way with words, and he made me feel like I was special. He called me his "sunshine." Other men visited me at home, brought me flowers, and tried to court me. But I felt nothing toward them. I had no interest in any of them. My heart belonged to Vic. I'd tell the suitors I had a boyfriend in California, and they replied that I wasn't married yet, so they were not going away. But I gave Vic the key to my heart. While I was turning down suitors and remained faithful to Vic; he was a young bachelor, going out on dates in his new home, Los Angeles. He was a player; he dated left and right. After we got married, he told me that he was uncertain about us while we had our long-distance courtship. He was worried that I would just "drop him" anytime.

Six months after we met, Vic proposed in a letter and said he wanted to spend the rest of his life with me. We spoke on the phone, and he confirmed that he was serious. I was nervous about my life completely changing. I knew I loved this man but didn't know what life would be like to leave my family and everyone I knew in the Philippines to go to California. In October 1971, I replied in a letter, "Yes."

We continued our long-distance relationship until he came back to the Philippines in December of 1972 and we got married in January 1973. We wanted to get married in December, but my brother, Vicente, got married that same month. It's a Filipino superstition not to marry in the same year as your family members, so we moved our wedding to New Year's Day. The wedding preparation took less than a month from choosing the wedding dress to the location, to finding the reception. Together, we visited family members and friends and delivered the wedding invitations. I was twenty-three, and he was twenty-eight. We were young and in love.

Vic graduated with a degree in foreign affairs from Lyceum University. He then worked at Subic Naval Base in Olongapo, Philippines, and worked in human resources. He was always proud that he could hire his friends and townmates. He provided jobs to his community, and I admired that about him. He loved to sing and dance. He took advantage of any opportunity he had to hold the mic. Wherever he was, he had to be the emcee. He made me laugh with his jokes and he thought I was easy to please. Vic was determined and persistent. He didn't stop pursuing me until I said *yes*.

CHAPTER 5

Life in the USA

When I landed in Los Angeles, Vic introduced me to his coworkers and friends who had also recently moved from the Philippines. They were newly married and just beginning to start a family. We all arrived around the same time, and we experienced similar challenges as new Filipino immigrants in America. Before having children, we would spend time exploring the city. He took me out on dates to the movies and to sights in LA. Before I started working, I stayed at home and performed the tasks of what I thought an "ideal" wife would do. I cooked, cleaned the house, washed clothes, and even ironed his underwear, while waiting for him to come home. I was happy I got to take care of him. Being a dutiful housewife did not last long. I was bored with staying at home and wanted something else to do, so I went to look for a job. While I took public transportation, I would see Hispanic children on the bus. They reminded me of my nephews and nieces that I missed in the Philippines. As a young couple in the United States, Vic and I went to amusement parks, like Disneyland and Universal Studios. We always took Vic's nieces and nephews Melinda, Mel, and Charity with us. They were the children of his oldest brother, Maning, and his wife, Cel, and we loved having them with us.

My first job in the United States was with a water company next to the Los Angeles Airport, where I worked as an accountant. During that time, I was the only Asian in an all-white staff. Though I was different from my peers, I was welcomed and accepted. I focused my efforts on doing good work as an accountant. I would take the bus from Los Angeles to my job, which was about an hour commute going there. I worked there less than a year and became pregnant. While I was at the office, I went to the bathroom and noticed I was losing a lot of blood. I was scared and sad. I knew I should not have been bleeding if I was pregnant. I went to the hospital the next day and the doctor told me I had a miscarriage. I was sad and scared. I didn't tell anyone but my husband. Vic and I thought it was because of my long commute, so we decided to move closer to my job. Within the same year, I got pregnant for the second time. We needed to move back to Los Angeles, because our apartment complex near my job prohibited children.

Vic was so excited about being a father. I was excited and nervous about being a mother. I didn't have my mother or sisters around to ask them questions about what to expect. I didn't know what to do. When I was pregnant with my first child and in my third trimester, I went to the emergency room at least five times, because I thought he was coming. I would mistake pain for contractions and would tell the nurses in the hospital, "I think he's coming out, I think he's coming out." The doctor would examine me and ask me to go home. As my first child was getting close to being born, I remember feeling so much pain. I screamed for hours while in labor, until the doctor finally gave me an epidural. It knocked me out. I was scared and excited to bring home our son, Voltaire Joseph, our first VJ. I had no idea how to raise a child. I didn't even know how to hold him. I didn't have my family close by to show me. I learned on my own as things came up. I relied on the pediatrician and other doctors if I felt something was wrong or had questions. When I was worried and didn't know why he would be crying for so long, I would call the doctor. He would tell me that I just needed to burp him.

Though I left my family in the Philippines, I gained Vic's family and friends in Los Angeles. They were a big support during our early years creating a family. We were able to rely on our networks for childcare, and a parent of a friend of the group was able to watch my firstborn, Voltaire. We would go to each other's houses and our children would play together. After I had Voltaire, I worked as a junior accountant for a famous singer, Ray Charles. I was proud I was able to work for a celebrity. His recording studio was in the same building where I worked.

CHAPTER 6

All My Children

WE GOT YOU BACK

Voltaire Joseph, a.k.a. VJ

Voltaire, being our first child, we did not have the slightest clue of what to do. I didn't have my mom or my sisters to help me take care of an infant. I learned it the hard way. I remember, when he was two, Vic and I were on our way to visit a friend. We were on the freeway. VJ was in the car seat in the back, I was sitting in the front passenger seat, and Voltaire would not stop crying. I did not know why. Vic needed to pull over to the side of the freeway. He picked Voltaire up from his car seat and carried him, walking with him along the side of the road to try to pacify him. Vic did this for fifteen minutes, and it worked. Voltaire calmed down, and they went back to the car. I waited in the car and was relieved that he stopped crying. Vic had the magic touch. VJ was two when we decided to buy our first house. It was a two-bedroom, one-bath house in Los Angeles, by Melrose and Beverly Boulevard. Vic and I were so excited; we had scrambled and worked many hours to make our first down payment.

When VJ was a teenager, it wasn't easy. He was stubborn like his dad. We wanted to raise VJ with our Filipino conservative values and culture, but VJ's American friends had more freedom and a relaxed curfew. Voltaire and Vic would butt heads, like any growing teen and a strict father. For VJ's sixteenth birthday, we had him choose between a drum set and a car, because of course, he wanted both. VJ's best friend was amazed that he chose a drum set. I think he knew he would get a car anyway. VJ used the drum set for a short time. I am not sure if he even took lessons, but I remember it rotting in the back patio. He also eventually got a car.

During our first trip to Hawaii, VJ was seventeen years old and chose not to come with us. Later we found out the reason was that he had artwork on his body, a.k.a. his first tattoo. He did not want us to see it. Three years later, I took him to a chiropractor to treat his back pain, and that's when I discovered his tattoo. I was not pleased. He tried to hide it, and I asked if he could get it scraped from his body. He said nothing.

Voltaire is an artist and loves to draw and paint. He studied graphic design and, as an adult, got a job working in television production and enjoyed working behind the scenes. VJ grew up to be a responsible, caring, and loving individual. He has a successful job in the film and TV industry that he loves and enjoys. My regret is that Vic is not physically around to witness and see what VJ has become. However, I think Vic is always here. I know Vic has not stopped guiding VJ and protecting him, and that is true for all our kids. Voltaire is currently a video engineer.

Victoria Virginia, a.k.a. Vicky Jean (Our Second VJ)

Two and a half years after I had Voltaire, I had my firstborn daughter, Victoria. This time, I knew what to expect. The pregnancy and the labor were a lot easier than with my first child. As a newborn, Vicky was able to sleep through the night. We ended up moving to San Fernando Valley, a big suburb of Los Angeles, before Vicky was born.

Being a mother was nerve-racking. When Victoria was eight years old, Vic and I took the kids to Malibu Beach with our relatives. We drove in three different cars that were packed with snacks and toys for the kids. It was a fun day playing on the beach and enjoying time with my relatives and kids. We all came back to the house and discovered that Victoria was left at the beach. I thought she was in another car with her cousins. I could feel my heart pounding when I found out she wasn't with us. I felt like the earth caved in and fell on me, not knowing where my daughter was. I sat in my family room, which I used as my home office, and called all the authorities I could think of. I finally reached one of the guard towers on the beach. Thank God, there was a guard at the gated beach, and Vicky was fortunately there. After learning what happened,

Vic immediately drove back and went to Malibu Beach in a hurry. One of our neighbors hopped on his motorcycle and rode to the beach as well.

Apparently, in the chaos of packing up all the cars, Vicky left the group to pick up VJ's sand toys that he left on the beach. When she came back, we were all gone. She started crying, and people were approaching her, asking if she was lost. She went to the bathroom to hide. When she came out, someone took her to the guardhouse where we were finally able to reunite with her. I was relieved.

Victoria was the responsible one. She was the peacemaker of all my children. She would stop fights between her quarreling siblings. While growing up, she excelled in everything she did. She graduated with honors from high school. She was president and homecoming queen of her senior class. Vicky went on to graduate from USC with a bachelor's degree in broadcast journalism. Vicky's first job was with *Larry King Live*, a world-renowned hit TV show on CNN. We were all very proud of Vicky's accomplishments at a young age. Vicky went on to become the supervising producer of *Dancing with the Stars*, and other reality shows like *The Bachelor* and *The Bachelorette*.

Her coworkers would tell me that she was hardworking and pleasant to work with.

Valerie Jo, a.k.a. Lori Jo (Our third VJ)

Vic was a good father. He was responsible, loving, and caring. While in labor with our third child, Vic had already been through this twice before and figured he had plenty of time to leave and grab coffee at the hospital. But by the time he returned to my hospital room, Valerie had already arrived! So Vic nicknamed her "Speedy Gonzalez."

While Valerie was just three months old, I was diagnosed with malignant cancer 1 of the thyroid. There was no pain, but it felt like a marble that would move up and down on the back of my throat. I was scared when I found out, and I was told I needed to get surgery to remove the cancer. The word *cancer* was scary. The first doctor who saw me didn't even examine me but saw the lump in my throat and concluded to have surgery. Going into surgery, I was terrified, but they successfully removed my thyroid gland to prevent the cancer from spreading. Fortunately, I had my aunt Mama Pacing and cousin Linda living with me at the time, and they helped me around the house while I was healing from the procedure. I needed to take a pill every day for the rest of my life. At the time, I had a newborn, a two-and-a-half-year-old, and a five-year-old.

They put a metal collar on me to hold my neck up during the healing process. I was only thirty years old, with three little ones, and survived my first major surgery and first bout with cancer. It was hard not to be able to hold my little ones. I was grateful that I had my family, my aunt Mama Pacing, and cousin Linda with me to help prepare meals for us and to help me take care of my three small children.

After I healed from surgery, I went to work for Universal Studios as a staff tour accountant. It was a big company and a very stable and secure job that had good pay and benefits. As the children were growing up, Vic and I realized the kids needed more attention. I quit my job and got my real estate license so I could have a more flexible schedule to be with them when I needed to. The ironic part of this career change was that I actually worked longer hours as a realtor, but it paid off. I had the flexible time that I wanted to raise our three children, and I was able to help my husband financially. We were fortunate enough to travel a lot with the family and were able to send our children to good private schools. At times I was working so hard, I felt like I was neglecting my kids, but I always thought that I was working hard to give them a good education and better life.

It was challenging to find a good babysitter to help raise my kids before they were in school. We had family members watch them and sometimes strangers from an agency. It was a struggle to find good help, but like all parents, we did the best we could to provide a good life for our family.

When Lori Jo (which is what I called her—and I still do) was in high school, I remember her watching a television show about teen pregnancy. A group of teen moms were sharing their experiences and challenges with being a parent. I was in the kitchen preparing dinner when Lori came running down the stairs to me, hugged me, and thanked me for being strict. She was grateful I instilled in them the Catholic values of waiting to have sex until after marriage. Lori Jo was the president of her junior high school class and was a tough cookie

Lori was loved by her friends and teachers. Lori drove our family Dodge van in high school. We called it the "Titanic," and she would take her friends from school to ride with her.

Valerie (Lori) completed her degree in business administration with an emphasis in marketing from California State University of Long Beach. Lori is currently a successful realtor working for a big franchise real estate company in Los Alamitos, California.

Vicky and Lori attended the same high school and were only two years apart in grades. They were known as the "Mercado Girls," and their male classmates liked the lunch that I would prepare for them and ask if they could have some of the Mercado lunch.

Veronica Jamie (our fourth and final VJ)

Seven years after I had my third child, Valerie, I found out I was pregnant again. We thought we were done after Valerie. The three children were demanding more of our time with their busy school activities combined with our busy work schedules. I didn't think I would be able to handle another child. I was not young anymore; I was thirty-six at the time. The doctors called pregnancy at this age "high-risk," and I was worried the child would be born with abnormalities because of my age. It was difficult to accept. Vic and I talked a lot about all the difficulties and challenges that came with raising another child, and we decided to terminate the pregnancy. My relationship with God was not as strong at that time, to even think of such a thing.

I remember calling Kaiser from a phone booth to inquire about the abortion process. I was told that the hospital didn't do that procedure. I was given a referral to a private clinic that offered abortions. We made an appointment and went to the clinic. It was full of young pregnant women who looked scared and by themselves. Vic and I were silent. I was nervous. I finally said, "My older sister, Lily, is going to be so upset if she finds out." With no discussions, I said, "We aren't going to do this." Vic agreed and we both stood up. We went to the nurse's desk to cancel the procedure. She said, "But you are the next in line." We didn't respond and just turned around and left.

From that day, we accepted Veronica, and we were so happy. We went through the next nine months like the happiest couple ever. It was like we were having our first child. We told our kids, and they had so much fun coming up with her name. We completed our Vs with Veronica. During the pregnancy, I wore the most beautiful maternity clothes and worked full time with no medical issues. I followed the doctor's prenatal recommendations, ate the right food, and exercised to have a happy and healthy baby. I thank God for allowing me to accept another gift of life. I thank God for continuing to bless me with love.

Veronica was always a good student. She graduated high school at Notre Dame with magna cum laude. She went to San Diego State University and got her degree in social work. She then went on to the University of Chicago and completed her master's degree in social service administration. She worked in Chicago for four years after graduate school as a community organizer. In 2016, after Vic passed away, Veronica moved back to California to be with me. She now lives in Los Angeles, California, and is a happy and successful wellness coach, environmental advocate, and community leader, transforming people's lives, helping them heal trauma and accomplish their dreams.

* * * * *

I thank God for blessing Vic and me with healthy, happy, and caring children. Being a mother is everything and stressful. Being a mother is indeed a significant role filled with love, joy, and fulfillment, but it can also be challenging and stressful at times. It's a roller coaster, and it's important to recognize and address the stress that comes with parenting in order to maintain well-being.

Vic and I were blessed to celebrate our twenty-fifth wedding anniversary in 1998. It was a significant milestone that we celebrated with loved ones. Having our families, friends, and relatives in attendance made the occasion even more special. Our anniversary celebration gave us an opportunity to reflect on the beautiful memories we created together and challenges we overcame. They were a time to appreciate and cherish the love and support we have received from our families, friends, and relatives.

CHAPTER 7

Career Woman

I worked as an accountant at Universal Studios–Los Angeles before obtaining my real estate license. Working as a realtor was a rewarding experience. Not only was I able to help my family with a financially lucrative career, I was also able to help other families achieve their dreams of becoming homeowners. After six years, I obtained my broker's license and later started my own real estate company. Then years after that, I opened my own mortgage brokerage, while Vic was still working for Pacific Bell, which is now AT&T. Vic retired at age fifty-eight and joined me in our real estate business. We were two peas in a pod. Working side by side, every day for a number of years. With God's blessing and support from my husband, I was an owner of several different franchise real estate companies, such as Realty World, Homelife, and Coldwell Banker Prime Properties

* * * * *

"There is only one thing that makes a dream impossible to achieve, the fear of failure."

"When we strive to become better than we are, everything around us becomes better, too."

"You are what you believe yourself to be."

"Don't allow your mind to tell your heart what to do."

—Paulo Coelho

Dec. 20, 2016

* * * * *

I was at the peak of my career when the market crashed in 2008. The real estate industry was heavily impacted. My business went under, along with many businesses, from big corporate banks to small independent businesses like mine. Many homeowners lost their homes. It was such a strain on families, who ended up filing for bankruptcy and even divorce. Some lost it all. They couldn't handle the stress and pressure of the loss; some even ended their lives. It was such a dark period for my colleagues and friends. I remember the water and power shut off our utilities in our office building because we weren't able to pay. We lost some of our rental properties, and our retirement funds dropped tremendously in value.

My husband and I were worried, yet we stayed strong in the face of difficulty with faith and hope. We worked harder and smarter. Our children were already out of the house and did not see the stress we went through. With the big losses and uncertainty, we were grateful for what we did have, the love we had for one another, and our children. We did not give up. We continued to work with the clients we had before the recession. Fortunately, there were new opportunities available to offer our services through short sales and foreclosures. We were able to gain new clients. We moved, along with many of my agents, to another Coldwell Banker office, Greater Valleys, now Coldwell Banker Exclusive, where I have been a Broker of Record since 2012. I currently supervise close to 170 agents.

CHAPTER 8

The Love of My Life

Vic was a hopeless romantic. When I first came to California, he took me to Echo Park, Los Angeles, and we walked around the lake, dreaming up our lives together. We loved traveling together. After having our fourth child, we finally took a first trip outside the United States. We went to Europe with a couple of friends to look at a business opportunity. I left my four kids ages twelve, nine, seven, and four months old newborn, with my sister Leonor and nephews Junjie and Manny. We went to London, England, and Paris, France. What is known to be the most romantic city in the world and in front of the Eiffel Tower, Vic and I had a huge argument. Not your ideal way to spend time in a romantic city, but that was part of being married. He loved taking pictures and seeing the sights. And one of those sights, in particular, was other women. I got so mad when I saw him taking pictures of other women, we argued. I stormed by myself and went back to the hotel. I was so upset. I started the bathtub and tried to drown myself. I knew I wasn't really going to do it, but I was so angry I wanted to show him how upset I was. He came in, worried, and pulled me out of the tub. We were finally able to calm down. During the rest of the time, we tried to make the best of our trip.

Throughout our marriage, we traveled the world together. We visited Switzerland, Germany, Russia,

Paris, London, Italy and Spain. Our trip to Spain was one of the most memorable trips. We had our three children and Vic's sister and brother-in-law with us to spend Christmas. During the family's shopping spree in Madrid, Vic got pickpocketed and his wallet was stolen. On Christmas Eve, my sister-in-law and her husband were mugged. What an experience in a foreign land. Thankfully, we were safe and we were together.

In our relationship, Vic never questioned my decisions or ambitions in life. He always supported me and believed I could do anything. I was able to accomplish getting my real estate license, my broker's license, and starting my own business because of his love and his belief that I could do anything I put my mind to. After our kids were grown and out of the house, Vic had retired from SBC, he would always bring me breakfast in the morning while I would be getting ready for work. He would bring me lunch at work.

Like any relationship, we had our ups and downs, including moments of conflict and disagreement, but we maintained a deep love for each other and never gave up on our relationship. This resilience and commitment are important qualities that contribute to the growth and strength of a partnership. Our love for one another and our family was a powerful force that helped us overcome challenges. Coming back to love helped us work through our differences. The arguments and disagreements didn't matter because we knew we wanted to be together. Through these difficult times, our relationship was tested, and we grew. We learned to understand and support each other.

To the couples, remember that open communication, mutual respect, and willingness to compromise are key ingredients in maintaining a healthy and thriving relationship. It's these qualities that allow couples to navigate conflicts and build a foundation of love and understanding.

In 2012, Vic showed his unconditional support. I had undergone radiation treatment for my right breast that had cancer, *cancer* no. 2. This was detected through mammography, then a biopsy was completed. Radiation treatment is a common treatment option for breast cancer. It is typically delivered externally using a machine, called a linear accelerator. Each session is usually painless and lasts only a few minutes. The treatment is typically given on a daily basis, Monday through Friday, for several weeks. Vic drove me every morning for thirty-one days for the treatment. I would go straight to the office after radiation and do my daily routine. I didn't tell anyone and no one else knew, not even our children. Thank God, the cancer was at its early stage.

A few years later, I was diagnosed with atrial fibrillation, a heart condition characterized by irregular and often rapid heartbeats. It caused symptoms like fatigue and shortness of breath. Managing this disease includes medications that I take every day to control the heart rhythm and reduce the risk of complications.

In 2015, I started to have difficulty breathing. It was necessary to put a pacemaker on me. It is a medical device to regulate my heart rhythm. It helps ensure that the heart beats at a normal rate and rhythm. The process of undergoing a pacemaker implantation did not take long. I remember Vic and Vicky who were supposed to wait while I was in the operating room, went to grab a bite to eat and by the time they came back, I was already at the recovery room. I remember the doctor mentioning that I was the youngest on the recovery floor.

CHAPTER 9

Losing Vic

A few months before Vic died, it seemed like he had a premonition or knew he wouldn't be with me for long. He kept telling people how lucky he was that I chose him. He told me how much he appreciated me and how lucky he was. I shrugged it off and told him, "Get out of here," we've been together for over forty-five years. He also kept bringing plants and fresh flowers home. After work, I would come home and tell him, "I want to cook for you." He would tell me not to. He wanted me to rest and not have to take care of him.

On June 10, 2016, Vic woke up in the middle of the night in pain. He was kneeling by the couch in front of our bed and called out to me. I woke up. He was pointing to the top of his head. I called 911 and told the dispatcher he had a severe headache. The first ambulance that came was not equipped for a stroke. We had to wait for a second ambulance; they came fifteen minutes later. When the first paramedic arrived, he asked Vic to say his name. Vic wasn't able to speak his name clearly, and his lips were deformed. The paramedic told me that he suspected Vic had a stroke. He was still alert when they picked him up. They put him on the stretcher and rushed him to the hospital. I drove myself to the hospital.

When I arrived, I wanted to see him, but I had to fill out forms and found out what happened from the hospital attendants. When I was finally able to see the doctor, they said that they took an X-ray of Vic and that blood went to his brain. Part of the brain was affected by the interruption of the oxygen supply, and it was inoperable. It didn't register what that meant for me at the time. When I saw him, I touched his face. He could feel it was me; he tried to sit up and then he collapsed. He fell over and he never woke up. Dealing with the death of my loving husband was an incredibly difficult and painful experience. Grieving is a unique and individual process, and it's important to allow yourself to mourn and heal in your own way.

A stroke is when a person has a sudden loss of oxygen in the brain. It is the third cause of death and the first cause of disability worldwide. Every year, fifteen million people suffer from a stroke, and six million do not survive. He was then unconscious in the hospital for seven days until he took his last breath. This is the same memory I have of when my father passed away when I was a teenager.

I was waiting by Vic's bedside every day, talking to him, praying that he would wake up.

After the passing of her husband, Queen Elizabeth famously said, "Grief is the price we pay for love." And I experienced this grief with the loss of my darling Vic. I loved him so much and felt like it was the end of the world, and I wanted to die. I wanted to follow him. When we finally went home, I was still in shock; I didn't know what to do or how to live. My oldest daughter, Vicky, might have sensed my pain. While I was washing the dishes one morning, which Vic loved to do because he couldn't stand seeing dirty dishes, Vicky came up to me and said that she wanted me to live and that I had grandchildren to live for.

The death of my husband on June 17, 2016, brought me and my children closer. I tried my best to be strong for them. During the first year of his death, I wrote letters to Vic. This was my way of talking to him. I never doubted his love for me. I knew he would do anything for me and his family.

The first year after his death was one of the hardest years of my life. I remember leaving the parking lot of my office alone and it brought me to tears, because Vic was not there to drive me home. He used to take me to meetings and drove me to work. We were like two peas in a pod and were always together. I missed Vic so much. I would visit Vic at the cemetery every day. It brought me life. I would sit in a lawn chair next to his site and talk to him and pray that he was happy and at peace. I made sure his headstone was perfect and would kneel down and trim the grass around it with scissors.

I went back to work quickly as a way to keep myself occupied and distracted during the difficult time. It was my therapy that kept me going. I found solace in staying busy and maintaining my routine. Others may need more time and space to process their emotions. Grief affects everyone differently, and there is no one-size-fits-all approach to mourn.

I must admit I had no clue why Vic was having a severe headache. I didn't know that was one of the signs of stroke.

Below is what I wish I knew.

What's the Difference Between a Heart Attack and a Stroke?
(The article below was posted in https://nwregionalheart.com/whats-the-difference-between-a-heart-attack-and-a-stroke on December 30, 2022.)

Heart attacks and strokes have quite a bit in common: They are both medical emergencies caused by a sudden cut-off in blood flow. In a heart attack, the blood flow to your heart is suddenly blocked. A stroke occurs because of a sudden interruption of blood flow in your brain. With both conditions, timely medical care is crucial for lowering the damage to your brain or heart.

Know the signs of stroke: Act FAST.

Other symptoms according to medical record:

- Numbness or weakness in your face or limbs, especially affecting only one side of the body
- Confusion, difficulty speaking or trouble understanding others
- Blurred or impaired vision in one or both eyes
- Dizziness, difficulty walking or balance problems.

Common heart attack symptoms:

- Chest pain, especially on the left side or center of your chest
- Discomfort that radiates from your chest through your shoulders or arms
- Jaw, neck, or back pain
- Feelings of fullness, pressure or squeezing in your chest

- Shortness of breath, even at rest
- Weakness or lightheadedness.

In the initial year after his passing, I wrote him daily letters, expressing my longing to hear from him.

CHAPTER 10

Grief and Sickness

A few months after Vic passed away, I had so many health issues. My daughter, Jamie, joked that I was her guinea pig as she was learning to be an energetic healer (which I'm still not quite sure what that is). A few months after Vic left this world, I experienced excruciating pain in my knees. I had never experienced that kind of pain in my life. It was Thanksgiving, and we were at my daughter Lori's house. After dinner, I could not bend my left knee. It was like a thousand needles penetrating my kneecaps. My daughter's husband, my son-in-law, Eric, suggested I try marijuana. He was using it to help him with pain in his knee. My youngest daughter, Jamie, took my grandkids to the other room, while my eldest son, Voltaire, daughter Lori, and her husband tried to teach me how to inhale marijuana from a pipe. Before that, I had never smoked or inhaled a cigarette, let alone weed. Unfortunately, I didn't feel anything. I don't think I was able to inhale it. The night progressed, and so did the pain. Jamie rushed me to the emergency room. They took an X-ray and said I had mild arthritis. The only consolation I felt at that time was that Vic never experienced that kind of pain. It was the first major holiday since Vic left, and I was sad and lonely. Perhaps the pain was a symptom of my depression.

A mass in my pelvis was discovered in 2017, just before my appendix burst and was removed. Around the holidays, I felt like I was in the most pain. I remember I attended an open house and felt pain and discomfort in my stomach. I didn't take it seriously and went on with my day. That same night, I woke up with severe pain, and I could not stand up straight. I waited until the next morning when the doctor's office was open to call them and let them know what I was experiencing. They told me to go straight to see my doctor. Jamie drove me, and during the drive, I remember each bump we drove over, I would scream. The sudden movement made my stomach feel worse. They did lab work and X-rayed my stomach. My doctor told me that my appendix had burst, which they said was one of the worst things that can happen. I was admitted to the hospital, and I needed surgery to remove my appendix. During surgery, they found a mucus substance that showed signs it could be cancer, so I was referred to an oncologist after the surgery to a different hospital. There, I found out that it was cancer of the appendix, cancer 3, which was a rare type of cancer that, they told me, only one in a million people would have. I struggled to accept it.

The doctors told me that I would need a laparoscopy, which involves a camera to give a proper diagnosis. They said I needed to undergo a hot wash chemo treatment to clean the area that was exposed to the cancer, so it doesn't spread to different parts of my body. I went to City of Hope to get a second opinion. They confirmed that a laparoscopy and hot wash chemo treatment were necessary. Between December 2017 and February 2018, I underwent two laparoscopy procedures. After I recuperated from my surgery, I went back to work. I still had medical bags emptying the excess fluid from my body when I went back to the office and saw my clients. I bought a new wardrobe of skirts so I could hide the medical pouches that were taped to me. I knew how to look good even though cancer was leaking from my body.

Dealing with cancer multiple times was incredibly challenging. I thank God for giving me strength in overcoming these challenges. I am grateful for the successful treatments and appreciate the gift of restored health. While cancer can bring many difficulties, it can also provide an opportunity for personal growth and a deeper appreciation for life. I cherish the moments of health and happiness and continue to live my life to the fullest.

Experiencing cancer multiple times can be an incredibly challenging and difficult journey, both physically and emotionally. Dealing with the diagnosis, treatments, and potential recurrences can take a toll on various aspects of one's life. To those who are suffering from cancer and other diseases, remember to take care of your overall health and well-being, including regular checkups and screenings, as well as adopting a healthy lifestyle that promotes prevention.

My name was given to me in honor of Our Lady of Lourdes. In 1858, Mary appeared in Lourdes, France, to Saint Bernadette, a fourteen-year-old peasant girl. Mary instructed her to dig in the ground nearby, from which came a spring of healing properties. This story makes me think of all the times that I recovered from my illnesses and survived, especially the time I lost a lot of blood and woke up from being unconscious. The doctor acted like it was a miracle. Perhaps Mary's healing miracle has been working through me through all my years.

CHAPTER 11

Life Began at 72

I wasn't ready to go. I didn't want to die. I didn't want my children to experience the grief they had gone through with Vic. I wanted to be with Vic, but I saw my children go through so much pain; I didn't want to see them go through it again.

After my last hospitalization and hearing from the doctor, "*We got you back,*" I haven't been back to the hospital for a major sickness since. I wasn't ready to leave this earth and felt *heaven could wait*. I felt my life begin again at seventy-two. I had a renewed energy after I realized I almost died. I wore my natural curly hair, which I hadn't done for over twenty years. I started cooking again and learned new culinary recipes. I started having a social life and went out more with friends and clients for lunch and dinner.

I volunteered in my parish and in our Lions Club International, where Vic was elected president in 2016–2017 but was not able to live out his presidency. In 2021–2022, I accepted the position of president for our Lions Club. During that time, our club became fifth out of fifty-five clubs in the district for its number of people served and funds donated. I even took up piano, a childhood dream of mine. In my first lesson, I played the song "You Are My Sunshine." In Vic's first postcard, he wrote to me, he said, "You are my sunshine." I know Vic still comes to me in small subtle ways when I don't expect it.

COVID

In January 2020, the coronavirus COVID-19 hit the world. In March, the California governor shut down the state, and the city's stay-at-home policy was officially in place. I thought because of my medical issues, if I got COVID, it would be the end of my life. Before the vaccine was available, I was scared to leave the house. I moved my office to my home and worked from my house for four weeks. Just like many workers and business owners, I was conducting office meetings via Zoom and showing properties virtually. Though I went back to my office after a couple of months, I continued to work from home for two years. I would work in my pajamas from early morning till late in the evening, assisting borrowers in their home financing and supervising over eighty realtors remotely.

Many people experienced grief during the COVID-19 pandemic. Shock and disbelief were common reactions. The pandemic has brought immense sorrow and tragedy to countless lives around the world. I myself experienced grief at the loss of friends. Grieving the loss of someone is a complex and personal process. It's important to allow oneself to feel the pain and sadness that comes with such a loss.

It was devastating when my personal friend, Tessie's husband, Ricky, lost his life to COVID-19. It did not take very long; he was in the hospital for only nine days. No one could see him to even say goodbye. The family members were communicating with him through video up to his last breath. I expressed my condolences, reached out to her, and let her know that I was there. Fortunately, she is a strong woman and has children who love her so much and have a job that keeps her busy and occupied. In addition to her job, she is also busy volunteering to help the less fortunate in her community.

Losing a loved one is always a difficult and painful experience, and it can be especially challenging when it's a result of a global pandemic like COVID-19.

It was very scary when our family went to Canada for Christmas. My daughter Vicky, who is a resident of Canada, was tested positive a week before we came back to California, then followed by her husband and children. Fortunately, Lori's family and I tested negative before coming back. Upon arrival in California, my son-in-law and the youngest child were sick and tested positive, then followed by the rest of the members of the family. Fortunately, I was not affected and still COVID-free—"COVID virgin" as they say.

May 19, 2023, I attended the Lions Club convention of District 4L3 in Las Vegas. I attended the talent show where I impersonated Elvis Presley, the boldest and most entertaining act I've ever done. The King of Rock 'n' Roll had a charismatic stage presence and iconic style, so it was an exciting performance. It was fantastic that I was able to surprise and impress the audience with my moves. It was even more special when my loved ones were there to support me and cheered me on. My youngest daughter, Jamie, encouraged me and provided tips for my routine. My second child, Vicky, flew all the way from Canada. VJ and Lori flew from California to be there. My sister-in-law Louella and her husband, Fernando from Las Vegas, were there too to give their support. Their support made a significant difference in boosting my confidence.

Impersonating Elvis Presley and performing such an iconic dance routine took courage and a passion for entertaining. It was wonderful that I enjoyed the experience and embraced the stage without feeling nervous or shy. I had a memorable time and made a lasting impression on the audience. It was a bold and successful act.

LOURDES "LULU" R. MERCADO

Relationship with God

The nature of one's relationship with God is deeply personal and can depend on an individual's beliefs, religious affiliations, and personal experiences. I was born a Catholic and grew up Catholic. Prayer and worship are common ways to engage in a relationship with God. Worship involves reverence, adoration, and devotion to God. Some people experience a sense of God's presence and guidance in their everyday lives. Others find strength in their relationship with God during challenging times, seeking comfort, hope and spiritual support.

I am engaged more in regular and heartfelt prayer. Shared my thoughts, desires, struggles, and gratitude with God. I know Lord Jesus and His Mother, Virgin Mary, listen and care about every aspect of my life.

*****

When I find myself in times of trouble
Mother Mary comes to me
Speaking words of wisdom, let it be

—Beatles

I always desire to intellectually share my religious beliefs with others. It can be a meaningful engaging experience. To do so, I need to do the following.

1. Respect others' different perspectives and beliefs. Listen actively to others as well.
2. Share personal experiences. I should take time to explain how my beliefs have made an impact on others' lives in a positive way, which can make my message relatable.
3. Be informed. I desire to learn about other religions and worldviews to better engage in meaningful dialogues.

I surround myself with a supportive community of believers. I seek opportunities to serve others. Engaging in acts of kindness and selflessness through my involvement with Lions Club and my church community not only benefits those around me but also strengthens my relationship with God.

Chrismas, 2022

Christmas, 2015.
Last family photo with Vic

Lulu at home April 2024

Lulu- Jan. 2024- In the cruise ship,

Lulu- one of the recipients of WOW (Woman of Worth Awards) of 2022

Lulu photo with VJ

With Vic, when he was installed President
of Fil Am Lions Club in 2005.

On our 25th wedding anniversary in 1998

President and owner of a real estate franchise.

With Vic and grandchildren

2024 Mother's Day in Hamilton,
Canada with grandchildren

Canada vacation

With my children

On one of my birthdays in Long Beach with Lori and VJ

Ethan's team won 1st place in a Basketball tournament.

Christmas time in Canada

Charlie and Ethan with Auntie Jamie

GIVING

I slept and dreamt that life was joy. I awoke and
saw that life was service. I acted and behold,
Service was joy.
—Rabindranath Tagore

According to the *Bhagavad Gita*, "Through selfless service, you will always be fruitful and find the fulfillment of your desires. This is the promise of the Creator."

I am truly blessed with my children and grandchildren. I thank Vic for his active participation and involvement in raising our children.

I thank God for the treatment of my multiple cancers.

It is important to celebrate these victories and acknowledge the strength and determination it took to face each battle.

ACKNOWLEDGMENT

I would like to take a moment to express my deepest gratitude to my darling husband in heaven and my incredible family; my eldest son, Voltaire (VJ), and his partner, Crystal; Joaquin and Jonah; daughter Victoria and her husband, Greg, and their children—Gavin, Miles and Saige; my third child, Valerie, her husband, Eric, and their children—Ethan, Charlie and Cooper. I would like to thank my youngest daughter, Veronica Jamie, who helped and encouraged me to write this book along with Victoria.

I am truly blessed to have each and every one of you in my life. You have been my pillars of strength, unwavering support, and endless love.

Together, we have weathered storms, celebrated triumphs, experienced, and overcome countless hurdles. It is through our collective experiences and the love we share that I have grown into the person I am today.

Life has thrown its fair share of challenges at us, but it is through these hardships that our bonds have grown stronger.

Your unwavering faith in me, your encouragement, and your belief in my abilities have helped me move forward, even in the face of adversity.

Thank you for being my rock, my cheerleaders, and my source of strength. I am forever grateful for your love. Without you, I would not be the person I am today.

I want to thank my brothers and sisters and the people that I worked with and continue to work with who have supported me in my difficult times. I want to thank my business partners who were always there and continue to trust me.

With my love and gratitude,
Lourdes "Lulu" R. Mercado

ABOUT THE AUTHOR

"Lourdes "Lulu" R. Mercado, a Filipina, immigrated to America to be with her husband, Vic, where they started a family of four children. However, life presented its share of challenges.

Amidst a recession, Lulu courageously battled three cancers and faced a near-death experience—a perilous sight. Yet, she remained resolute, determined to continue living, fulfill her purpose, and give back. Her resilience and inner strength were awe-inspiring, serving as a true inspiration when her story was recounted. She steadfastly refused to let illness dictate her destiny, embracing each day without hesitation.

Lulu firmly believed that her life held more to offer; her unwavering spirit and positive energy inspiring those around her to thrive.

Her narrative serves as a powerful reminder: never surrender. Keep forging ahead, regardless of obstacles. Lulu's journey stands as a testament to living life to the fullest, demonstrating that even after a fall, one can rise again."

Printed in the USA
CPSIA information can be obtained
at www.ICGtesting.com
LVHW070626091024
793248LV00019B/389